The Compleat New England Huswife

System of the whole Art and Mystery
of Goody's Cookery

To my Aunt Betsy

Acknowledgements

My thanks to the following people who gave generously of their time and enthusiasm and made this book possible with their library treasures.

James Z. Kyprianos, John Whipple House of 1655, The Ipswich Historical Society

Marilyn Corning, The Claflin-Richards House of 1650 to 1660, Wenham Museum

Don Daly, Pioneer Village in Salem

Marshall Swan, The Castle of 1715, The Sandy Bay Historical Society of Rockport

Elizabeth Tinsley, Parson Barnard House 1715 and the Johnson Cottage, 1789, North Andover Historical Society

The Staff in the Library of the Essex Institute, Salem, Massachusetts

Back cover illustration from Mrs. Dalrymple's handwritten recipes, 1795, reproduced by kind permission of the Essex Institute, Salem, Massachusetts

Design and typesetting by Alison Anholt-White
© 1992 Albion Press

The Compleat
New England Huswife

System of the whole Art and Mystery of Goody's Cookery

Being a Collection of *Ancient and Approved* Recipes

Flesh, Fish, & Fowl	Sauces
Soops & Stews	Sallets & Potherbs
Dairy	Puddings
Baking	Sweetmeates
Brews	Preserves

To which is added
Instructions for the **NOVICE** for
Roasting & Baking, and Boiling,
household *Hints,* and good *Advice*

Researched and compiled by
Elizabeth Stuart Gibson

Kissing don't last, cookery do.
George Meredith

From the Preface to
The Compleat Housewife, or the Accomplish'd
Gentlewoman's Companion, E. Smith, 1729

These Receipts are all suitable to English Constitutions & English Palates, wholesome, toothsome, all practical and easy to be performed. Here are those proper for a frugal, and also for a sumptuous Table, and if rightly observed, will prevent the spoiling of many a good Dish of Meat, the Waste of many good Materials, the Vexation that frequently attends such Mismanagement, and the Curses not infrequently bestowed on Cooks with the usual Reflection, that whereas God sends good Meat, the Devil sends Cooks.

❦❦❦

From the Preface to *The Accomplish'd Cook, or the*
Art and Mystery of Cooking, Robert May, 1685

It is impossible for any Author to please
all People, no more than the best Cook
can fancy their Palats whose Mouths
are always out of taste.

Of Roasting – General Rules
to be observed

Mrs. Ann Partridge, 1725, The New and Complete Universal Cook, or the Young Woman's Best Guide to the Whole Art of Cooking

Your fire must be made in proportion to the joint you are to dress: that is, if it be a little or thin piece, make a small brisk fire, that it may be done quick and nice: but if a large joint, lay a good fire to cake, and let it be always clear at the bottom. Allowing a quarter of an hour for every pound of meat at a regular fire, your expectations will hardly ever fail, from the largest to the smallest joint.

Of roasting *Beef*

Mrs. Ann Partridge, 1725, The New and Complete Universal Cook

If it be a furloin or chump, butter a piece of writing paper, and fasten it on the back of your meat with small skewers, and lay it down to a soaking fire at a proper distance. As soon as your meat is warm. dust on some flour, and baste it with butter, then sprinkle some salt, and at times baste with what drips from it. About a quarter of an hour before you take it up, remove the paper, dust on a little flour, and baste it with a little butter, that it may go to table with good froth. Garnish your dish with scraped horseradish and serve it up with potatoes, broccoli, French beans, cauliflower, horseradish, or celery.

Meat in the home is a great source of harmony.

William Cobbett, Cottage Economy

🍎🍎🍎

**You can have fresh meat frequently, even in warm
weather, if when you kill a sheep or calf you pass it
around to the neighbors, and they return the
Compliment when they kill. It is usually safer to wait
for cool Weather before killing beef and pork, for by
so doing you can have them the year round. Freeze
what you need for winter use. Put down a barrel of
pork and another of beef, and when spring comes,
why, there you are! Fowls are always to be had.**

Several Ladies, 1805, The Pocumtuc Housewife

Of roasting a *Turkey, Goose, Duck, Fowl, &c.*

Amelia Simmons, 1796, American Cookery

When you roast a Turkey, Goose, Fowl, or Chicken, lay
them down to a good Fire. Singe them clean with white
Paper, baste them with Butter and dust on some Flour. As
to time, a large Turkey will take an Hour and twenty
Minutes, a middling one a full Hour: a full grown Goose, if
young, an hour: a large Fowl three quarters of an Hour, a
middling one half an hour and a small Chicken twenty
minutes, but this depends entirely on the Goodness of
your Fire.

When your Fowls are thoroughly plump, and the
Smoke draws from the Breast to the Fire, you may be sure
that they are very near done. Then baste them with Butter:
dust on a very little Flour, and as soon as they have good
Froth, serve them up.

🍎🍎🍎

**Don Daly of Pioneer Village in Salem, Mass-
achusetts, when asked how a large turkey could cook
in an hour and and half, said, "The large wild turkey
was about this big." Then he held out his hands as if
holding a basketball.**

Rosting *Lobster*

Elizabeth Wainwright, 1711, The Receipt Book of a Lady of the Reign of Queen Ann

Strech ye lobster & tey it upon ye spit a live & if you do not wash it before you spit it you must do it after wt water and solt. Yn set a plate under it to catch ye gravey and bast it with eather butter or clarid & put ye gravey to best butter for ye sauce. Let it be prety thick & send it on a plate by it self. A large one will take a qutr of an hour.

NOTE: This recipe which requires skewering a live lobster might be the reason lobster was such an unpopular food in Massachusetts in colonial days.

Rosting *Eel*

E. Smith, 1729, The Compleat Housewife or Accomplish'd Gentlewoman's Companion

Take a large Eel, and score him well with Salt; then skin him almost to the Tail; then gut and wash, and dry him, then take a quarter of a pound of suet shred as fine as possible, put to it sweet-herb and eschalot likewise, shred very fine and mix it together with some Salt, Pepper, grated Nutmeg, scotch your Eel on both sides the breadth of a Finger's distance and wash it with yolks of Eggs and strew some Seasoning over it and stuff the Belly with it; then draw the skin over and put in a long skewer through it and tye it to a Spit and baste it with Butter and make the Sauce Anchovy and Butter melted.

Some families like to get up a great dinner on Sundays and have friends who drive to Meeting from a distance come in for the Nooning. There is no objection to this if everything is prepared the day before. The meat should be plain Roast so that it can be started and left. A young child can tend the Spit while the rest of the family is away.

Several Ladies, 1805, The Pocumtuc Housewife

Sauces

To *Enhance your Rost*

Mrs Ann Partridge, 1725, The New and Complete Universal Cook

Geese and Ducks are commonly seasoned with Onions, Sage, and little Pepper and Salt. A Turkey when roasted is generally stuffed in the Craw with Force-meat or the following Stuffing. Take a Pound of Veal, as much grated Bread, half a Pound of Suet cut and beat very fine, a little Parsley, with small Matter of Thyme, or Savory, two Cloves, half a Nutmeg grated, a Teaspoonful of shred lemon Peel, a little Pepper and Salt, and the Yolks of two Eggs.

Sauce for a Turkey – Good Gravy in a Boat, and either Bread, Onion, or Oyster-sauce in a Bason.
Sauce for a Gander – A little good Gravy in Boat, Applesauce in a Bason and Mustard.
Sauce for a Goose - Same as for the Gander.
Sauce for a Fowl - Parsley and Butter or Gravy in the Dish, and either Bread, Sauce, Oyster Sauce, or Egg Sauce in a Bason.

To *Farce all Things*

Thomas Dawson, 1597, The Second Part of the Good Hus-wives Jewell

Take a good handfull of Tyme, Isope, Parselye, and three or foure yolkes of Eggs hard Rosted, and choppe them with Hearbes small, then take white bread grated and raw egs with sweet butter, a few small Raisons, or Barberies, seasoning it with Pepper, Cloves, Mace, Sinamon and Ginger, working it altogether as Paste, and then may you stuffe with it what you will.

Sauce for a Stubble Goose

Markham, 1683, The English Housewife

Take the pap of roasted apples and mixing it with Vinegar, boil them together on the fire with some of the gravy of the goose and a few Barberries and bread crumbs when it is boiled to a good thickness season it with sugar, and a little cinnamon, and so serve it forth.

Sauce for *Land-fowl*

Robert May, 1685, The Accomplish'd Cook

Puree one teacup of boiled prunes, drained, and stoned, one teacup pan gravy from roasting chicken, 1/2 teaspoon ground cinnamon, 1/4 teaspoon ground ginger, 2 Tablespoons sugar, salt, and serve hot with roast chicken.

English Ketchup

E. Smith, 1729, The Compleat Housewife

Take a wide mouthed Bottle put therin a pint of the best White-wine Vinegar: then put in ten or twelve Cloves of Escalot peeled and just bruised: then take a quarter of a pint of the best Langoon White-wine; boil it a little, and put to it twelve or fourteen anchovies washed and shred and dissolve them in the Wine, and when cold put them in the Bottle, them take a quarter of a pint more of White-wine and put in it Mace, Ginger, sliced, and four Cloves, a spoonful of whole Pepper just bruised. Let them boil all a little; when near cold, slice in almost a whole Nutmeg, and some Lemon-peel, and likewise put in two or three spoonfuls of Horseradish; then stop it close, and for a Week shake it once or twice a day; then use it; 'tis good to put in to Fish Sauce or any savory Dish of Meat; you may add to it the clear Liquor that comes from Mushrooms.

❦❦❦

Garlicks tho' used by the French are better adapted to the uses of medicine than cookery.

Amelia Simmons, 1796, American Cookery

Mushroom Catsup

Mrs. Dalrymple's Handwritten Recipes from 1795

As soon as the mushrooms are gathered I put a layering of them first, then a layering of salt in a pan after remaining in this state for a week squeeze them through a cloth, boil the liquor with cloves, allspice, mace, nutmeg until all the scum has risen when it is cool bottle tight, sufficiently so to exclude air. It is sometimes necessary to boil it over next year.

To make a *Horseradish Sauce*

Sir Kenelme Digbie, 1669, The Closet Opened

Mix a half teacup grated horseradish, 2 tablespoons of vinegar, and two teaspoon of sugar, and serve with roast beef.

❦❦❦

To do a fine hanged beef – the piece that is fit to do is the Navel piece and let it hang in your Cellar as long as you dare for stinking.......

E. Smith, 1729, The Compleat Housewife

To make a *Cucumber Sauce* for *Mutton*

E. Smith, 1729, The Compleat Housewife

To fry Cucumber for Mutton Sauce, you must brown some Butter in a Pan, and cut the Cucumber in their slices; drain them from the Water, then fling them into the Pan, and when they are fried brown, put in a little Pepper, and Salt, a bit of an Onion, and Gravy, and let them stew together, and squeeze in some Juice of Lemon, shake them well, and put them under your Mutton.

To make *Green Sauce for Broil'd Eel*

Patrick Lamb, 1716, Royal Cooking

Pound some Sorrel and squeeze out the Juice. Then cut an Onion very small, and toss it up with Butter and minc'd Capers: mix with it your Juice of Sorrel: squeeze in an Orange and add some pepper and salt.

NOTE: this should do well on any seafood.

Mustard of Dijon or French Mustard

Robert May, 1685, The Accomplish'd Cook

The seed being cleaned stamp it in a mortar with vinegar and honey then take eight ounces of seed, two ounces of cinemon, two of honey, and vinegar as much as will serve good mustard not too thick, and keep it close covered in little oyster-barrels.

"For a man seldom thinks with more ernestness of anything than he does of his dinner."

Samuel Johnson

11

Frying

**Joseph Ingersoll, in his will of 1757, listed all his
earthly, personal possessions to be:**

One bellows

Glasses and earthenware

One chair, two chests and old pots

One old frying pan

*Joseph lived at cellar hole #19 which can be found at Dogtown in
the wilds of Cape Ann, Massachusetts.*

To fry *Salt Cod Fish*

Several Ladies, 1805, The Pocumtuc Housewife

Soak cod fish over night in cold water. Cut into pieces
about two inches square, roll in Indian meal and fry with
salt pork.

To fry Eels

Mrs. Ann Partridge, 1725, The New and Universal Cook

After having skinned and cleaned your eel split them
and cut them in pieces let them lay for two or three hours
in a pickle made of vinegar, salt, pepper, bay leaves, sliced
onion, and juice of limons then drudge them with flour
and fry them in clarified butter – serve them dry with fried
parsley and lemon for garnish. Send plain butter and
anchovy-sauce in separate cups.

Haddock

**"You clean the innards out, 'an you cut the head off;
and that's all. You don't never bone 'em nor
split them."**

New England Cook Book of Fine Old Yankee Recipes

To fry *Chickens*

Lucy Emerson, 1808, The New England Cookery

Cut your chickens in pieces, half boil them with slices of pork in water sufficient to cover them, then take gravy from the pan and fry them in butter till they are light brown: then add the gravy with a spoonful or two of sweet wine nutmeg and salt thicken it with flour. Garnish with sippets within the dish.

❧❧❧

**Pavica, a Goodwife from Pioneer Village
in Salem, advises,**

"It is wise to bank your coals of the fire together to save for the morning. Make a little heap in a warm place of fire and cover it with ashes from around. Make the cover about 1 to 1 1/2" thick. You don't want smoke and you don't want it to go out. More coals require more ash to cover."

To spitchcock *Eels*

Susannah Carter, 1796, The Frugal Housewife or Compleat Woman Cook

You must split a large eel down the back and joint the bones cut it in two or three pieces melt a little butter put in a little vinegar & salt let your eel lay it it two or three minutes, then take the pieces up one by one, turn then round with a little fine skewer roll them in crumbs of bread & broil them of a fine brown. Let your sauce be plain butter with the juice of lemon or good gravy with an anchovy in it.

Of Boiling – General Rules
to be Observed

Mrs. Ann Partridge, 1725, The New and Universal Cook or the Young Woman's Best Guide in the Whole Art of Cooking

Be sure that your pots and covers are well tinned, very clean, and free from sand. Mind that your pot really boils all the while else you will be disappointed in dressing any joint though it has been a proper time over the fire. Fresh meat must be put in when the water boils, and salt meat whilst it is cold. Take care likewise to have sufficient room and water in the pot, and allow a quarter of an hour to every pound of meat, let it weigh more or less.

Boiled Dinner

Several Ladies, 1805, The Pocumtuc Housewife

First make sure the fire is good and steady, such as will last until Dinner is served. As soon as breakfast is well out of the way, hang on the big pot half full of cold water, and put in a piece of corned beef and a chunk of salt pork. About nine, if the water is boiling hard, put in the pudding, being careful that the cloth has been dipped in scalding water, squeezed dry and floured, before the pudding is placed in it. Put in the beets about the same time. At half past ten put in the cabbage, at eleven carrots and turnips, and at half-past eleven parsnips and potatoes, and squash in quarters on top. Serve the pudding first with butter and molasses. Then dish up the dinner, with the beef and pork in the middle of the platter and the vegetables arranged around them in a tasty manner.

To boil a *Calf's Head*

Mrs. Ann Partridge, 1725, The New and Universal Cook

The head must be picked very clean, and soaked in a large pan of water a considerable time before it be put into the pot. Tie the brains up in a rag and put them into the pot at the same time with the head; skim the pot well, then put in a piece of bacon in proportion to the number of people to eat thereof. You will find it to be enough by the tenderness of the flesh about that part that joined to the neck. When enough, you may grill it before the fire or serve it up with melted butter bacon, & greens and with the brains mashed and beat up with a little butter, salt, pepper, vinegar, or lemon, sage, and parsley in a separate plate; and the tongue slit and laid on the same plate; or serve the brains whole and the tongue slit down the middle.

NOTE: If this book were larger, it would include a recipe for each part of the animal. Robert May, 1685, The Accomplish'd Cook, includes the following:

To boil Oxe-Cheeks
To dress Oxe Cheek Otherways
To marinate Oxe Cheek
To dress Noses and Lips of any Beast, Steer Oxe, or Calf
To make Black Puddings of Beefers Blood
To make Udders either in Pie or Pastry
To bake a Heifer's Udder in the Italian Fashion

To boil a *Capon or Chicken with Spargas*

Robert May, 1685, The Accomplish'd Cook

Boil your capons or chicken in fair water and some salt, then put in their bellies a little mace, chopped parsley, and sweet butter; being boiled serve them on sippets and put a little broth on them then have a bundle or two of spargas boil'd put in beaten butter, and serve it on your capon or chicken.

To boil a *Cod's Head*

Mrs. Ann Partridge, 1725, The New and Universal Cook

After tying your cod's head round with pack thread to keep it from flying, put in a fish-kettle on the fire large enough to cover it with water: put in some salt, a little vinegar, and some horse-radish slice: when the water boils, lay your fish upon a drainer, and put it into the kettle, let it boil gently till it rises to the surface of the water, which it will do if the kettle is large enough, then take it out, and set it to drain; slide it carefully off your drainer into your fish plate. Garnish with lemon and horseradish scraped. Have oyster sauce in one bason and shrimp in another.

Salt-Fish with Cream

Charles Carter, 1730, The Complete Practical Cook

Take good Barrel-Cod, and boil it, then take it all into Flakes, and put it in a Sauce-pan with Cream, and season it with a little Pepper; put in a Handful of Parsley scalded and minc'd and stove it gently till tender and then shake it together with some thick Butter and the Yolks of two or three Eggs and dish it and garnish with poached Eggs and Lemon sliced.

To boil *Scate*

Elizabeth Wainwright, 1711, The Receipt Book of a Lady of the Reign of Queen Ann

Great care must be taken in cleansing this fish; and as it is commonly too large to be boiled in a pan at once, the best way is to cut it into long flips crossways about an inch broad, and throw it into salt and water; and if the water boils quick it will be enough in three minutes. Drain it well and serve it up with butter and mustard in one bason and anchovy or soy sauce in another. You may, if you please, place spitchcocked eels round about the scate.

Soops & Stews

To make a *Gravy to keep for Use*

E. Smith, 1729, The Compleat Housewife, or Accomplish'd Gentlewoman's Companion

Take a piece of coarse Beef cover it with Water when it has boil'd some time take out the Meat, beat it very well, and cut it in pieces to let out the Gravy: then put it in again, with a bunch of Sweet-herbes, an Onion stuck with Cloves, a little Salt, some whole Pepper; let it stew, but not boil: when 'tis of a brown Colour 'tis enough; take it up, put it in an earthen Pot, and let it stand to cool; when tis cold scum off the Fat: it will keep a Week, unless the Weather be very hot.

To make a *Barley Broth*

Robert May, 1685, The Accomplish'd Cook, or the Art and Mystery of Cooking

Take a Chine or Knuckle, and joynt it, put it in a Pipkin with some strong broth, and when it boils, scum it, and put in some French Barley being first boiled in two or three waters with some large mace, and a faggot of sweet herbs bound up and close hard tied, some Raisins, Damask Prunes, and Currans, or Prunes, and Marigold-flowers, boil it to an indifferent thickness and serve it on sippets.

To make a *Soop*

E. Smith, 1729, The Compleat Housewife

Take a Leg of Beef, and boil it down with some salt, a bundle of Sweet-herbs, an Onion, a few Cloves, a bit of Nutmeg, boil three gallons of Water to one; then take two or three pounds of lean Beef cut in thin slices; then put in your Stew-pan a piece of Butter, as big as an Egg & flour it

& let the Pan be hot & shake it till the Butter be brown; them lay your Beef in your Pan over a pretty quick Fire, cover it close, give it a turn now & then, & strain in your strong Broth with a Anchovy or two a handful of Spinnage and Endive boiled green and drained and shred grosse, then have Pattels ready boiled and cut into pieces, Toast, fried and cut like dice, and Forc'd meat Balls fry'd. Take out the fry'd Beef and put all the rest together with a little Pepper and let it boil and quarter of an hour and serve it up with a Knuckle of Veal or a Fowl boil'd in the middle.

Mrs. Peabody's Pease Soup

Amelia Simmons, 1796, An American Cookbook

Pick and wash a quart of split peas add to them a gallon of water 2 lb of lean beef or use the water in which a shin of ham has been boiled 2 onions one head of celery washed clean, a sprig of sweet marjoram, half a teaspoonful of black pepper, parboil a piece of salt pork and put it into the soup half an hour before the soup is served strain it through a course sieve and then through a fine one, wash the pot and put back the soup.

Pease Porridge

McKendry, 1695, The Family Dictionary

Take Leg of Beef or other fresh Meat, and make of it strong Broth. Take two or three Quarts of hull'd Pease & boil them by themselves to a Pulp with little piece of Bacon; then take Sorrel, Spear Mint, & Parsley chopt put it into the strong Broth and stew it over some Coals with a quarter of a pound of Butter: Thicken it with the Pulp of the Pease, and stir it; when you put them together, put in some French bread with a little Salt, Pepper, and Butter when you eat it.

**Pease porridge Hot, Pease porridge Cold,
Pease porridge in the Pot, Nine Days Old**

Traditional Rhyme

Green Pea Soop

E. Smith, 1729, The Compleat Housewife

Take a half a bushel of the youngest Peas, divide the great from the small; boil the smallest in two quarts of Water, and the biggest in one quart: when they are well boiled, bruise the biggest and when the thin is drained from it, boil the thick in as much cold Water as will cover it: then rub away the skins, & take a little Spinnage, Mint, Sorrel, Lettuce, and Parsley, & and a good quantity of Marigolds, wash, shred, and boil these in half a pound of Butter, and drain the small Peas, save the Water and mingle all together, and a spoonful of Pepper whole, then melt a quarter of a pound of Butter and shake a little Flour into it and let it boil, put the Liquor to the Butter, and mingle all well together, and let them boil up. So serve it with dry'd bread.

English Potage

Sir Kenelme Digby, 1669, The Closet Opened

A good potage for dinner is thus made: boil beef, mutton, veal volaille and a little piece of the lean of gammon of the best bacon with some quartered onions and (a little) garlic, if you like it. You need no salt, if you have bacon, but put in a little pepper and cloves. If it be in the winter, put in a bouquet of sweet herbs, or whole onions, or cabbage. If seasonal of herbs, boil in a little of the broth apart, some lettuce, sorrel, borage, and bugloss, etc till they be only well mortified. If you put in any gravy, let it boil or stew a while with the broth: put it in due time upon the toasted bread to mittoner, etc. If you boil some half-roasted meat with your broth it will be better.

French Herb Pottage for Fasting Days

Robert May, 1685, The Accomplish'd Cook

Take half a handful of Lettuce as much of Spinnage, half as much of Bugloss and Borrage two handfuls of Sorrel, a little Parsley, Sage, and good handful of Purslane, half a pound of Butter, some Pepper, and Salt and sometimes some Cucumbers.

Meager Spring Pottage

Charles Carter, 1730, The Complete Practical Cook

First take spinach & sorrel parsley, lettice, and onions, boil all these down in fair water very well Season it with whole pepper, cloves, and mace, put in a good faggot of sweet herbs, French bread, a Manchet cut into slices: boil it well and strain it out, and force all the green and goodness through your strainer, and this is for your stock.

Then take spinach, sorrel, lettice, a little sellery and endive, a little parsley, and charvel, and some onions or leeks, and chop these, but not too small: then pass them in brown butter thickened until they are very tender: put to them some of your stock, as much as will fill you dish, stove it well, and then put a pint of cream and stove it a little longer, stove in it a whole manchet dic'd and put in: and at last beat up the yolks of six eggs in a little cream, and draw it up thick, and dish it with your loaf in the middle, garnish with scalded spinach and slic'd lemon, and serve it away hot.

Sop of Onions

Thomas Dawson, 1597, The Second Part of the Hus-wives Jewell

Take and slice your Onions, & put them in a frying panne with a dish or two of sweet butter and fire them together, the take a little faire water and put into it salt and peper, and so fire them together a little more, them boile them in a lyttle earthen pot, putting to it a lyttle water and sweet butter, &c. You may use Spinnage in like manner.

To boile *Onions*

Thomas Dawson, 1597, The Second Part of the Hus-wives Jewell

Take a good many onions and cut them in foure quarters, set them on the fire in as much water as you think will boyle them tender, and when they be clean skimmed, put in a good many of small raisins, halfe a spooneful of grose pepper, a good piece of Sugar, and a little Salte and when the Onions be thorough boiled, beat the yolke of a Egge with Vergious, and put into your pot and so serve it upon soppes. If you will, poch Egges and lay upon them.

🍎🍎🍎

Roger the Smythe of Pioneer Village in Salem, Massachusetts says, "If you have many fireplaces but have money to buy only one fireback, buy one for the fireplace in the kitchen. The fireback stores the fire's heat and releases it slowly and provides a good even heat for cooking."

Fireback made at Saugus Ironworks, Saugus, Massachusetts

Sallets & Potherbs

Of *all kinds of Garden Stuff*

Elizabeth Wainwright, 1711, The Receipt Book of a Lady of the Reign of Queen Anne

In dressing all sort of kitchen garden herbs, take care that they are clean washed: that there be no small snails or caterpillars between the leaves; and those that have received any injury by the weather, be taken off. Next wash them in a good deal of water and put them into a cullender to drain. Care must likewise be taken that your pot or saucepan be clean, well-trimmed, and free from sand or grease.

A Spinnach Sallet Boiled

1615, The Newe Book of Cookerie

Parboil Spinnach and chop it fine with the back of two chopping knives, then set it on a chafing dish of coals with Butter and Vinegar. Season it with Cinnamon, Ginger, Sugar, and a few parboiled Currants, cut hard eggs into quarters to garnish it withal and serve it upon sippets of toast.

A Sallet of Fennell

William Tabisha, 1675, The Whole Body of Cookery Dissected

Take young Fennel, about a span long in the spring, tye it up in bunches as do Sparragrass; when your Skillet boyle, put in enough to make a dish; when it is boyled and drained, dish it up as you do Sparragrass, pour on butter and vinegar and send it up.

A Grand Sallet

Robert May, 1685, The Accomplish'd Cook

Take green purslane and pick it leaf by leaf, wash it, and swing it in a napkin then being dished in a fair clean dish and finely piled up in a heap in the midst of it ly round about the centre of the sallett, pickled capers, currans, and raisins of the sun, washed, pickled, mingl'd and laid round it, about them some carved cucumbers in slices or halves, and laid round also. Then garnish the dish brims with borage, or clove jelly-flowers or otherways with jagged cucumber-peels, cloves, capers, and raisins of the sun, then the best sallet-oyl and wine vinegar.

A Sallet of all Kinds of Herbs

Thomas Jenner, 1653, A Book of Fruits and Flowers

Take your Herbs (as the tops of red Sage, Mint, Lettuce, Violets, Marigold, Spinach, & cetera) and pick them very fine in fair water; and wash your flowers by themselves and swing them in a strainer. Then mingle them in a dish with Cucumbers and Lemons pared and sliced: scrape thereon Sugar and put into Vinegar and Oil. Spread your Flowers on top of the Sallet, and take Eggs boiled hard and lay them about the dish.

A Tarte of Spinnage or of Wheat Leaves or of Colewortes

Thomas Dawson, 1597, The Second Part of The Good Hus-wives Jewell

Take three handfull of Spinnage, boile it in faire water, when it is boyled, put away the water from it and put the spinnage in a stone morter, grind it smal with two dishes of butter melted and foure rawe egges all to beaten, then straine it and season it with Sugar, Sinamon, and Ginger, lay it in your Coffin, when it is hardened in the oven, then bake it and when it is enough, serve it upon a faire dish, and cast upon it Sugar and Biskets.

❧❧❧

Lettuce maketh a pleasant sallat being eaten raw with vinegar, oile, and little salt: but it be boiled it sooner disgested, and nourisheth more. Lettuce may be eated at the end or the beginning of a meal: for being taken before meat it doth many times stir up appetite: and eaten after supper it keepeth away druckennesse which commeth by the wine: and that is the reason that it staieth the vapour from rising up into the head.

John Gerard, 1636, Gerard's Herbal

Baked Beans

Several Ladies, 1805, The Pocumtuc Housewife

Beans should be put in cold water and hung over the fire the night before they are baked. In the morning they should be put in a colander and rinsed. Then put back in kettle with a piece of pork. Streaked pork, fat and lean is most suitable. Slash the rind. Keep them scalding hot for an hour. Add pepper and salt, a tablespoon of molasses, a little mustard, and put them in the bean-pot and bake as long as you can, not less than three or four hours.

Of *Jerusalem Artichoke*

John Gerard, 1636, Gerard's Herbal. Here Gerard quotes John Goodyear of 17 October 1621

These roots are dressed divers ways, some boile them in water, and after stew them with sacke and butter, adding a little ginger. Others bake them in pies putting Marrow, Dates, Ginger, Raisin of the sun, Sack, &c. Others some other way as they are led by their skill in Cookerie. But in my judgment, which way so ever they be drest and eaten, they are a meat more fit for swine, than men.

❧❧❧

All Vegetables will remain green if boiled with cooking soda.

**Asparagus must be dried and immersed in boiling
water backwards (i.e. bunched and set in water
standing upright with the heads protruding
from the water).**

Apicius, 30 AD, Cookery and Dining in Imperial Rome

NOTE: *Joseph Vehling, in his translation of Apicius in 1936,
comments, "All medieval food literature of the continent and
indeed the early cookery books of England prior to La Varenne,
Le Cuisinier Francois, 1654, are deeply influenced by Apicius."*

To make *Fried Beets*

Patrick Lamb, 1716, Royal Cooking or the Compleat Court-Cook

Beets are a sort of Root, that for being common out not
to be despis'd: they are eaten either in Salads or fry'd in
the following manner. Having baked them in an Oven, peel
them, and cut them in Slivers long-ways, and of the
thickness of half an inch or rather more. The large ones,
when cut, are almost of the shape of Soles. Then steep
them in a thin Batter, made of white Wine, the finest
Wheat-Flower, Cream, the White and Yolk of Eggs (more
yolk than White) Pepper Salt & Cloves beaten to powder.
When they have lain in the Batter a little while, take them
out and drudge them with Flower, crumm'd Bread and
shred Parsly; Then fry them and when they are dry, serve
them in plates or small Dishes with Juice of Lemon.

Of *Pompions, &c*

John Josselyn, 1672, New England Rarities

Slice them when ripe and cut them into dice, and so fill
a pot with them of two or three gallons, and stew them
upon a gentle fire a whole day, and as they sink, fill again
with fresh Pompions, not putting liquor to them; and when
it is stewed enough, it will look like bak'd Apples; then dish,
puting butter to it and a little vinegar (with some Spice, as
Ginger, &c) which makes it tart like an Apple, and so serve
it up to be eaten with Fish or Flesh.

To keep *Green Peas till Christmas*

E. Smith, 1729, The Compleat Housewife

Shell what quantity you please of young Peas; put them in the Pot when the Water boils; let them have four or five walms, then first pour them into a Colander and them spread a Cloth on a Table, and put them on that and dry them well in it: Have Bottles ready dry'd and fill them to the Necks and pour over them melted Mutton fat, and cork them down very close, that no Air come to them.

Sit them in your Cellar and when you use them, put them into boiling Water with a spoonful of fine Sugar and a good piece of Butter; when they are enough drain and butter them.

Of *Corn*

John Evelyn Esq., 1699, Discourse of Sallets

It is light of digestion, and the English (i.e. the New Englanders) make a kind of Loblolly of it to eat with Milk which they call Sampe; they beat it in a Morter and sift the flower out of it; the remainder they call Homminey, which they put into a Pot of two or three Gallons with Water and boyl it upon a gentle fire till it be like a Hasty Pudden; they put of this into Milk, and so eat it. Their Bread also they make of the Homminey so boiled, and mix their Flower with it, cast it into a deep Bason in which they form the loaf, and then turn it out upon the Peel, and presently put it into the Oven before it spreads abroad; and the Flower makes excellent Puddens.

Another Opinion on Corn

John Gerard, 1636, Gerard's Herbal

It is of hard digestion, and yeeldeth to the body little or no nourishment. We have as yet no certaine proofe or experience concerning the vertues of the kinde of Corne: although the barbarous Indians, which know no better, are constrained to make a vertue of necessitie, and thinke it a good food: whereas we may easily judge, that it nourisheth but little and is of hard and evill digestion, a more convenient food for swine than for man.

🍎🍎🍎

In his small leather bound book which could fit into a back hip pocket, Andrew Riggs of Riggs Point in Gloucester kept track of his personal accounts of day work from 1719–1752. Some of the entries during 1747–1748 were as follows:

To half a days work	£2/00/0
To won bushel of corn	£1/00/0
To shearing sheep	7/0
To 30 bushels holing from the harbor	£2/04/0
To won daes work holing wood	£3/00/0
To won dae and half	£6/00/0
To won pound of honey	£0/04/0

NOTE: *His rates for holing (or hauling) varied; however, his well paid half day was at a rate better than today's minimum wage of $4.25 an hour. He bought a bushel of corn for two hours work. At a farm stand in Danvers, Massachusetts a bushel of corn in season in 1991 cost $13.*

Dairy

There be many mischiefs and inconvenience which may happen to butter in the churning, because it is a body of much tenderness, and neither will endure much heat not much cold for if it be overtreated, it will look white, crumble, and be bitter in taste; and if it be over-cold it will not come at all but will make you waste much labour in vain.

Markham, 1683, The English Housewife

Making Butter

E. Smith, 1729, The Compleat Housewife

As soon as you have milked, strain your Milk into a Pot and stir it often for a half an hour, then put it in your Pans or Trays: when 'tis creamed skim it exceeding clear from the Milk and put your Cream into an earthen Pot, and if you do not churn immediately for Butter, shift your Cream once in twelve hours into another clean scalded pot and if you find any Milk at the bottom of the Pot, put it away; and when you have churned wash your Butter in three or four Waters and then salt it as you would have it and beat it well, but not wash it after 'tis settled; let it stand in a Wedge, if it be to pot, till the next morning, and beat it again, and make your Layers the thickness of three Fingers and then strew a little Salt on it and so do till your Pot is full.

A charm to make butter come: repeat it three times.

Come, butter come
Come butter come
Peter stands at the gate
Waiting for a buttered cake
Come butter come

Adfy, 1655, A Candle in the Dark

Keeping Butter

Several Ladies, 1805, The Pocumtuc Housewife

To have sweet butter in dog days and through the vegetable seasons, send stone pots to honest, neat dairy people, and procure it packed down in May, and let them be brought in in the night or cool rainy mornings, and partake of no heat from the horse, and set the pots in the coldest part of your cellar.

Keeping Eggs

Several Ladies, 1805, The Pocumtuc Housewife

One pint of coarse salt, one pint of unslaked lime, to a pail of water. Eggs will keep sound and wholesome for years in this, if kept in a cool place.

Testing Eggs

Amelia Simmons, 1796, American Cookery

The best possible method of ascertaining freshness is to put the egg in water, if they lye on the bilge, they are good and fresh – if they bob up on end they are stale, and if they rise they are addled, proved, and of no use.

To broil *Eggs*

Robert May, 1685, The Accomplish'd Cook or the Art and Mystery of Cooking

Take an oven peel, heat it red hot & blow off the dust, break eggs on it and put them into a hot oven, or brown them on top with a red hot fire shovel, being finely broil'd put them in a clean dish with some gravy a little grated nutmeg and elder vinegar, or pepper vinegar, juyce of orange, and grated nutmeg on them.

To make *a Sugar Amlet*

Patrick Lamb, 1716, Royal Cooking

Beat up the Whites of a dozen Eggs and put the Yolks to them, together with some Lemon-peel shred very small: Add to it a little Cream and salt. Beat it all well together, and fry your Amlet. Before you turn it into the Dish, drudge it with Sugar in the pan, and let the brown Side lie upper-most in the dish, in which you first lay a Plate turn'd up-side down. Then powder it with some Sugar and candy'd Lemon-peel, shred very small: and at the same time glaze it with a red-hot Fire-shovel, and serve it hot.

Eggs to Frigacy

McKendry, 1695, The Family Dictionary

Take 12 Eggs, boil them hard, cut them into Quarters: to which put a Pint of strong Gravy and half a pint of white Port Wine. Season with a Blade or two of Mace, bruised Pepper, and a little Salt. Scald a little Spinage to make them look green, with a Pint of Oister's to lay around the Dish. Put the Eggs in the Stewpan with a few Mushrooms and Oisters and rowl up a piece of Butter in the Yolk of a Egg and Flower it up thick for sauce, Garnish with crisp Sippets, Limon, and Parsley. It is a nice side dish.

To fry *Eggs*

Robert May, 1685, The Accomplish'd Cook

Take fifteen eggs and beat them in a dish then have interlarded bacon cut into square bits like dice and fry them with chopped onions and put to them cream, nutmeg, cloves, and cinamon, pepper, and sweet herbs, chopped small (or not herbs nor spice) being fried serve them on a clear dish with sugar and juyce of orange.

The exactest Twenty-One Ways to the Dressing of Eggs

Robert May, 1685, The Accomplish'd Cook

The Tenth Way – Mince herbs, small, as lettice, bugloss, or borage, sorrel juyce or vinegar and some grated nutmeg and serve them on a dish with sippets.

The One and Twentieth Way – Slice some apples and onions, fry them but not too much, and beat some six or eight eggs with some salt put them to the apples and onions and make an omelet ring fried make some sauce with vinegar or grape-verjuyce butter sugar and mustard.

Thick Cream-Cheese

E. Smith, 1729, The Compleat Housewife

Take the Morning's Milk from the Cow and the Cream of the Night's Milk and Runnet, pretty cool together, and when 'tis come, make it pretty much in the Cheese-fat and in a little Salt and make the Cheese thick in a deep Mold, or a Melon Mold, if you have one; keep it a year and half or two years before you cut it. It must be well salted on the outside.

After old coats, panteloons, &c have been cut up for boys and are no longer capable of being converted into garments, cut them into strips and employ the leisure moments of children or domestics in sewing and braiding them for door mats.

Mrs. Child, 1832, The American Frugal Housewife, dedicated to those who are not ashamed of economy

Cheddar-Cheese

E. Smith, 1729, The Compleat Housewife

Take the new Milk of twelve Cows in the Morning and the Evening Cream of twelve Cows and put to it three spoonfuls of Runnet and when 'tis well wheyed, break it again, and work into the Curd three pounds of fresh Butter, and put in your Press, and turn it in the Press very often for an hour or more; and change the Cloths and wash them every time you change them; you may put wet Cloth at first to them but toward the last put two or three fine dry cloths to them; let it lie thirty or forty hours in the Press according to the thickness.

❦❦❦

Woollens should be washed in very hot suds, and not rinsed. Lukewarm water shrinks them.

Mrs. Child, 1832, The American Frugal Housewife, dedicated to those who are not ashamed of economy

❦❦❦

It is a good plan to put new earthen ware into cold water, and let it heat gradually, until it boils then cooled again. Brown earthen ware, in particular, may be toughened in this way. A handful of Rye, or wheat bran thrown in whole while it is boiling, will preserve the glazing, so that it will not be destroyed by acid or salt.

Mrs. Child, 1832, The American Frugal Housewife

Puddings

A Nice, Baked Indian Pudding

Lucy Emerson, 1808, New England Cooking

No. 1 Three pints scalded milk, 7 spoons fine Indian meal, stir well together while hot let stand till cooled: add seven eggs, half pound raisins, 4 ounces butter, spice, and sugar, bake one and a half hour.

No. 2 Three pints scalded milk to one pint meal settled; cool, add 2 eggs, 4 ounces butter, sugar or molasses and spice; it will require two and a half hours baking.

No. 3 Salt a pint meal, wet with one quart of milk sweeten and put into a strong cloth, brass or bell metal vessel, stone or earthen pot, secure from wet and boil 12 hours.

New Bedford Pudding

Mrs. Putnam's Recipe Book, and a Young Housekeeper's Assistant, 1810

Take four table-spoonsful of flour and flour of Indian meal, a little salt, & a cup of molasses: stir the other ingrediants into the milk and bake it three hours.

Ginger Pudding

Mrs. Dalrymple of Salem, Mass. Handwritten Receipts, 1795

3 pts milk make a batter as thick as for a common flour pudding, 1 qt. chopped apples, lb. suet, 3 gill molasses, large spoon ginger, a little salt. Boil 5 hrs.

Hedg-Hog Pudding

Esther C. Mack Industrial School, What Salem Dames Cooked, Recipe from 1683

Put some Raisin of the Sun into a deep wooden Dish and then take some grated bread, and one pint of sweet Cream, three yolks of Eggs, with two of the whites, and some Beef Suet, grated Nutmeg, and Salt. Then sweeten it with sugar, and temper it all well together, and so lay it into the dish upon the Raisins uppermost and then stick blanched Almonds very thick upon the pudding, then melt some butter and pour it upon the pudding, then strew some sugar about the dish and serve it.

Hasty Pudding

Several Ladies, 1805, The Pocumtuc Housewife

Put on water according to the size of your family. Sift five or six spoonfuls of meal into a bowl of water, and when the kettle boils, stir it in and let it boil up thick. Then stand over the kettle and sprinkle in meal, handful after handful, stirring it thoroughly all the time. When it is so thick the pudding stick stands up in it, it is about right. Cook half an hour. Eat it with milk or molasses. Either Indian meal or rye meal may be used. Rye hasty pudding and West Indian molasses as a diet, would save many a one the horrors of dyspepsia.

To make *Bread Puddings, yellow or green*

Robert May, 1685, The Accomplish'd Cook

Grate four penny loaves, and searce them through a cullender, put them in a deep dish, and put to them four eggs, two quarts of cream, cloves, mace, and some saffron, salt, rose-water, sugar, currans, a pound of beef-suet minced, and a pound of dates.

If green, juyces of spinage and all manner of sweet herbs stamped amongst the spinage, and strain the juyce, sweet herbs chopped very small, cream, cinnamon, nutmeg, salt, and other things, as is next before said; Your herbs must be time stripped, savory, sweet marjoram, rosemary, parsley, pennyroyal, dates in these seven or eight yolks of eggs.

NOTE: *If this is not green, it is yellow.*

Carrot Pudding

E. Smith, 1729, The Compleat Housewife

Take raw Carrots, and scrape them clean, grate them with a Grater without a back. To half a pound of Carrot take a pound of grated Bread, a Nutmeg, a little Cinamon, a very little Salt, half a pound of Sugar, a half a pint of Sack, eight Eggs, a pound of Butter melted, and as much Cream as will mix it well together; stir it and beat it well up, and put it in a Dish to bake; put Puff-paste at the bottom of your Dish.

Whortleberry (Blueberry) Puddings

Mrs. Putnam's Receipt Book

I – Take a pint of milk, three eggs, and flour enough to make a stiff batter. Stir them well together then add three pints of berries, flour a cloth, tie it pretty close, & boil it two hours & a half. Serve with wine sauce.

II – One cup of molasses one of milk one teaspoonful of salt & flour enough to make a thick batter; Stir in as many berries as will mix in the batter, boil it four hours. Serve it with sweet sauce.

Lemon Pudding

Mrs. Gardiner of Boston, Receipts from 1763

Take the Yolks of 8 Eggs well beaten, & the whites of only 4 of them, the Rhinds of 2 lemons grated & the Juice of one of them, somewhat less than half a pound of white Sugar, & a quarter of a pound of Butter. Mix all well together & bake it half an hour.

Marjoram Pudding

Eliza Smith, 1753 Edition, The Compleat Housewife

Take the curd of a quart of milk finely broken, a good handful of sweet marjoram chopt as small as dust, and mingle with the curd five eggs, but three whites, beaten with rosewater, some nutmeg and sugar, and half a pint of cream; beat all these well together, and put in three quarters of a pound of melted butter; put a thin sheet of paste at the bottom of the dish; then pour in your pudding, and with a spur cut out little slips of paste the breadth of a little finger, and lay them over cross and cross in large diamonds; put some small bits of butter on the top, and bake it.

❦❦❦

Majoram Pudding is old fashion, and not good.

E. Smith, 1729 Edition, The Compleat Housewife

To make *a Tansy*

Sir Kenelme Digby, 1669, The Closet Opened

Take three pints of Cream, fourteen New-laid eggs (the whites of seven put away) one pint of juice of Spinnach, six or seven spoonfuls of juice of Tansy, a Nutmeg (or two) grated small, half a pound of sugar and a little salt. Beat all these well together, then fry it in a pan with no more Butter than is necessary. When it is enough, serve it up with juice of Orange or slices of Lemon upon it.

Baking

Heating the Oven

Several Ladies, 1805, The Pocumtuc Housewife

Some people consider it economical to heat Ovens with fagots, brush, and light stuff. Hard wood heats it quicker and hotter. Take four foot wood split fine, and pile it criss-cross so as to nearly fill the oven, and keep putting in. A Roaring fire for an hour or more is usually enough. The top and side will at first be covered with black soot. See that it is all burned off. Rake the coals over the bottom of the Ovens and let them lie a minute. Then sweep it out clean. If you can hold your hand inside while you count Forty it is about right for flour bread; to count twenty is right for Rye and Indian. If it is too hot, wet an old broom two or three times and turn it round near the top of the oven till it dries; this prevents pies and cake from scorching on top. When you go into a new house, heat your oven two or three times to get it seasoned, before you use it.

37

Bake the Brown bread first, then flour bread and Pies, then Cake or puddings, and last Custards. After everything else is out put in a pan of apples. Next morning they will be deliciously baked. A pot of Beans can be baking back side, out of the way with the Rest.

If bread runs short before baking day comes, light cakes can be baked in the bake Kettle or the tin Baker. Draw out a solid mass of coals, set the bake-kettle over it, put in your biscuit, put on the lid, and cover with a thick layer of coals.

Pavica, Goodwife in Pioneer Village in Salem, says, "Have four or five hours of a raging fire to make the coals for your oven. In a dutch oven with coals on the bottom and coals on the top, pies take from an hour to an hour and fifteen minutes and cornbread half an hour".

Boston Brown Bread, to be baked in a Brick Oven

Mary H. Cornelius, 1830, Young Housekeeper's Friend Cookbook

Take a quart of rye meal and the same of fine Indian meal. (If this is bitter, scald it before mixing it with the rye. If it is sweet and fresh, almost every thing in which it is used is lighter without its being scalded.) Mix with warm water, a gill of molasses, a teaspoonful of saleratus, a large teaspoonful of salt, and a half a gill of yeast. Such bread is improved by the addition of a gill of boiled pumpkins or winter squash. Make it stiff as can easily be stirred. Grease a deep brown pan, thickly and put the bread in it, and dip your hand in water and smooth over the top. This will rise faster than other bread and should not be made over night, in the summer. If put into the oven in the forenoon it will be ready for the tea-table. In in the afternoon, let it stand in the oven till morning.

It is bad luck to cut bread at both ends of the loaf – never leave a knife stuck in a loaf — to drop bread on the floor accidentally is a good sign and a wish made when it is picked up —to drop bread butter side down means bad luck.

To make *Travelling Loaves*

Charles Carter, 1730, The Complete Practical Cook

Take Chicken or Pullets, Pheasants, or Partridges or Rabbet, and a Neck of Mutton or Lamb and roast it off cold, and cut your Fowl in Joints, and your Mutton into cullets: take large French Loaves of three Pence apiece, or other Bread; cut a Hole in the Top, and scoop out most Part of the Crumb, you may put fowl into one Loaf, Mutton, or Lamb into another, a Salad-Mogundy into another and sliced Ham and Tongue into another, putting a little Salt in a Paper with your fresh Meat: and as you travel you may eat anywhere on the Road in your Coach, carrying some Bottles of Drink, likewise, so, in haste, you may eat on the Road without staying by the Way.

To make *an Umble Pie*

Susannah Carter, 1796, The Frugal Housewife

Take the umblers of a buck, boil them and chop them as small as meat for minced pies, put to them as much beef suet, eight apples, half a pound of sugar, a pound and a half of currants, a little salt, some mace, cloves, nutmeg, & a little pepper, them mix them together, and put into a paste, add half a pint of sack, the juice of one lemon & orange, close the pie, & when it its baked, serve it up.

"Disguise if as you will, flavor it as you will, call it what you will, umble pie is umble pie, and nothing else."
Lowell, McClellan, or Lincoln

Of *Johnny Cake or HoeCake*

Lucy Emerson, 1808, The New England Cookery

Scald 1 pint of milk and put to 3 pints of Indian Meal and half pint flower – bake before the fire or scald with milk two thirds of the Indian meal, or wet two thirds with boiling water, add salt, molasses and shortening work up with cold water pretty stiff, and bake.

Indian Loaf

Mary H. Cornelius, 1830, Young Housekeeper's Friend Cookbook

To one quart of sweet milk put a gill of molasses, a teaspoonful of saleratus, a heaping pint of Indian meal, a gill of flour and a teaspoon full of salt, Stir it well together, put in into a deep brown pan and bake in a brick oven. It should be stirred the last thing before being set into the oven. It must be in the oven many hours at least eight or nine and if set in towards night should stand till morning.

❦❦❦

Indian Meal and rye meal are in danger of fermenting in summer; particularly Indian. They should be kept in a cool place, and stirred open to air once in a while. A large stone put in the middle of a barrel of meal, is a good thing to keep it cool.

Flapjacks

Mrs Dalrymple's Handwritten Receipts, 1795

1 qt milk 5 eggs 1 cup Indian meal 1 handful flour, stiffen with Rye meal

French Toast

Robert May, 1685, The Accomplish'd Cook, or the Art and Mystery of Cooking

Cut French bread and toast it in pretty thick toasts on a clean gridiron, and serve them steeped in claret, sack, or any wine, with sugar and juyce of orange.

❦❦❦

Hot bread is unwholesome to any man for it doth lie in the stomach like a sponge: yet the smell of new bread is comfortable to the head and the heart.

Muffins

Mrs Dalrymple's Handwritten Receipts, 1795

3 lb flour 1/2 pint yeast (not bitter) 6 whites eggs a little salt 1 qt new milk warm beat it with your hand 1/4 of an hour let it rise over night

Cinnamon Toast

Robert May, 1685, The Accomplish'd Cook, or the Art and Mystery Cooking

Cut fine thin toasts, then roast them on a gridiron, and lay them in racks in a dish, put to them fine beaten cinamon mixed with sugar, and some claret, warm them over the fire, and serve them hot.

Andrew Boorde, Dietary of Health, 1547

🍎🍎🍎

Nehemian Stanwood, a Weaver in Gloucester, Massachusetts, left his goodwife Sarah one fourth of his estate in his will of 1784. As stated in the document, Sarah inherited

one lower room in the western end of the said deceased dwelling House with a privilege to bake in the Oven in the Eastern Room of said House also the privilege of one Quarter part of the cellar; also one Cow right in the Pasture adjourning Said Dwelling and Village Land & as privilege to the Well the whole amounting to 20 pounds

NOTE: *Nehemiah was trying to be fair. I hope the arrangement was satisfactory on baking day.*

Sweetmeates

"A fat kitchen maketh a lean will."

Benjamin Franklin

Apple Pie

Lucy Emerson, 1808, The New England Cookery

Stew and strain the apples. To every three pints grate the peal of a fresh lemon, add cinnamon, mace, rose-water, and sugar to your taste - and bake in your paste. Every species of fruit such as pears, plums, raspberry, black berries may only be sweetened, without spices, and bake in paste #3.

Pompion Pie

Recipe from 1626, Wenham Museum's Colonial Receipts

Take about half a pound of pompion and slice it, a handful of Tyme, a little Rosemary, Parsley, and Sweet Marjoram slipped off the stalkes, and chop them small, than take cinnamon, nutmeg, pepper and six cloves, and beat them, take 10 eggs and beat them, them mix them and beat together, and put in as much sugar as you think fit, then fry them like a froiz, after it is fired, let stand til it be cold, then fill your Pye, take sliced apples thinne rounde wayes, and lay a row of the Froiz and layer or apples with currants betwixt the layer while your Pye is fitted, and put in a good deal of sweet butter before you close it; when the Pye is baked take six yolkes of eggs, some white wine or Vergis, and make a caudle of this, but not too thick, cut up the Lid and put it in, stir well together whilst the eggs and Pompions be not perceived and so serve it up.

Reverend Edward Holyoke of Marblehead kept a careful diary which is now in reprint form and called The Holyoke Diaries. This excerpt is his full record from January through July, 1742.

Jan 6 1742 Rev. Mr. Bradstreet died this Dec 26 buried today (Rev Simon Bradstreet of Charleston, father of this new minister at Marblehead)

7   My clock cleaned and time piece.

8   Went to Spencer

10   Preached at Ipswich Hamlet

11   Heard Mr. Noyes preach at Ipswich

15   Returned Home

21   Mrs. Epes came to town.

28   Mrs. Epes went home.

March 8 The snow 3 feet High in many streets in Boston

16   Went to Ipswich

17   I was married to Mrs. Epes
           (Mary Whipple, widow of Maj. Symond Epes of
           Ipswich)

29   Returned home

April 5   Sister Arnold went Home to live at Boston

July 24   Paid Mr. Turner 40/- entrance for Peggy for
           dancing school and to pay 60/- per quarter

Wedding Cake

Mrs. Dalrymple's Handwritten Receipts, 1795

10 lb flour, 10 sugar, 20 currants, 8 butter, 90 eggs, 1oz mace, 2 oz nutmeg, 1/2 pt rose water, 1/2 pt brandy

After the wedding ceremony has been performed at home by a magistrate in a simple civil ceremony... then a small celebration followed – not a great feast but a modest wedding dinner with bridal cakes and a cup of sack posset.

David Hackett Fischer, 1989, Albion's Seed

Mrs. P. Dodges Gingerbread

Mrs. Dalrymple's Handwritten Receipts from 1795

3 lb flour, 2 1/4 Sugar, 1 1/3 butter, 14 eggs, 1 1/3 gill rose water, 1 cup ginger spice

Rosewater

Several Ladies, 1805, The Pocumtuc Housewife

Pick rose leaves when they are in full blossom. Put a peck of them to a quart of water in a cold still over a slow fire and distill very gradually. Bottle the water, let it stand three days and cork it close.

French Cake to eat hot

E. Smith, 1729, The Compleat Housewife, or the Accomplish'd Gentlewoman's Companion

Take a dozen of Eggs and a quart of Cream and as much Flour as will make it into a thick Batter; put into it a pound of melted Butter, half a pint of Sack (sherry) one Nutmeg grated, mix it well and let it stand three or four hours then bake it in a quick Oven and when you take it out slit it in two and pour a pound of Butter over it melted with Rose-water; cover it with the other half and serve it up hot.

Shrewsbury Cakes

Elizabeth Wainwright, 1711, The Receipt Book of a Lady of the Reign of Queen Ann

A pd of flower, & 1 and half pd of Sugar, half pd of Butter a couple of Eggs, mix all together then roll it and cut it out with a drinking glass and so bake it upon tins.

❧❧❧

The Cat, by putting her Foot over her Ear when washing her face, fore shows Rain.

Worlidge, 1697, Systema Agriculturae

Littel Sugar Cakes

Elizabeth Wainwright, 1711, The Receipt Book of a Lady of the Reign of Queen Ann

Wegh a Pound of Flower after it is well dryd a Pound of Sugar finely beaten a Pound of fresh Butter, break the Butter in to the Flower and sugar and rub them very well together, take 2 Eggs the Whits of 4, beat ym very well with 3 or 4 spoonfuls of Rosewater. Put them to yr past and beat it with your hand half an houre you may put Corans in som but first plump them leave out as much butter as will butter your pans and bake them in a quick oven.

An Ordinary Cake to eat with Butter

E. Smith, 1729, The Compleat Housewife

Take two pounds of Flour, and rub into it half a pound of Butter, then put to it some Spice, a little Salt, a quarter and half of Sugar, and half a pound of Raisins stoned and half a pound of Currants; make these into a Cake with half a pint of Ale-yeast and four eggs and as much warm Milk as you see convenient: mix it well together, an hour an half will bake it. This Cake is good to eat with Butter for Breakfast.

A Modern Complaint

"Who can wonder that there is no health in the world when our very wheat–flour, sugar, and salt are adulterated with plaster of Paris, alum, and sulphate of copper....."

Mrs Horace Mann, 1857, Christianity in the Kitchen, a Physiological Cook Book

Two Plain Cakes

Lucy Emerson, 1808, The New England Cookery

I – Nine pound of flour 3 pound of sugar 3 pound of butter, 1 quart emptins, 1 quart milk, 9 eggs, 1 ounce of spice, 1 gill of rose water, 1 gill of wine
II –Three quarters of a pound of sugar, 1 pound of butter, and 6 eggs worked into 1 pound of flour.

Cheesecake

Wolley, 1664, The Cook's Guide

Set some Cream over the Fire and turn it with Sack and Eggs then drain it well and season it well with Rose-water and Sugar and Eggs, Spice, Currants and a few spoonfuls of Cream and put it into your crust adding a little Salt & so bake them.

NOTE: *Cheese is optional.*

March-pane

E. Smith, 1729, The Compleat Housewife

Take a pound of Jordan Almonds, blanch and beat them in a marble Mortar very fine; then put to them three quarters of a pound of double refined Sugar and beat with them a few Drops of Orange-flower-water; beat all together till 'tis a very good Paste, then roll it into what shape you please; dust a little fine Sugar under it as you roll it to keep it from sticking. To ice it, searce double refined Sugar as fine a Flour, wet it with Rose water and mix it well together, and with a Brush or bunch of Feathers spread it ovr your March-pan. Bake them in an Oven that is not too hot; put Wafer paper at the bottom and white Paper under that to keep them for use.

Plumb Cake

E. Smith, 1729, The Compleat Housewife

Take five pounds of fine Flour, and put to it half a pound of Sugar; and of Nutmegs, Cloves, and Mace finely beaten, of each half an ounce, and a little Salt, mix these well together, then take a quart of Cream, let it boil, and take it off, and cut into it three pounds of fresh Butter, let it stand still 'tis melted, and when 'tis blood warm, mix with it a quart of Ale-yeast, and a pint of Sack, and twenty Eggs, ten whites, well beaten, put six pounds of Currents to your Flour, and make a hole in the middle and pour in the Milk and other things and make up you Cake mixing it well with your Hands cover it warm and set it before the Fire to rise for half and hour, a then put it in the Hoop, if the oven be hot, two hours will bake it, the oven must be quick; you may perfume it with Ambergreese or put Sweetmeates in it if you please. Ice it when cold and paper it up.

In summer do not stir cake with the hand; the warmth of it make it less light. A wooden spoon kept on purpose is the best thing.

Mary Cornelius, 1830, Young Housekeeper's Friend

Tipcy Cake

Mrs. Putnam's Receipt book & Young Housekeeper's Assistant, 1810

Bake a sponge cake in a mould, blanch a handful of almonds, split them in four pieces and stick the cake full of them; set it in a deep glass dish, turn over it as much white wine as the cake will absorb & let it stand as hour turn in as much soft custard as the dish will hold.

Two Election Cakes

Mrs Dalrymple's Handwritten Receipts from 1795
I – 7lb flour, 2 butter, 2 1/2 sugar, 18 eggs, 1 qt 1/2 pt milk spice to your taste.
II – 10 lb flour, 8 butter, 4 sugar, 29 eggs, 3 pts yeast,
1 1/2 pt new milk, cinnamon, nutmeg, few cloves

Election Day was a spring event held on a Wednesday in April when the Charter of Massachusetts required that members of the Bay Company should meet to elect their officers. Gradually this day became a Puritan holiday which was celebrated with sermons and a ritual meal of Election cake and Election beer.

David Hackett Fischer, 1989, Albion's Seed

Whipt Cream

E. Smith, 1729, The Compleat Housewife,

Take a quart of thick Cream, and the whites of eight eggs beated with half a pint of Sack (sherry); mix it together, and sweeten it to your Taste with double-refined Sugar: You may perfume it if you please with some Musk or Ambergreese tied in a Rag and steeped a little in the Cream: whip it up with a Whisk, and a bit of Lemon-peel tied in the middle of the Whisk; take the Froth with a Spoon, and lay it in your Glasses or Basons.

Icing

Wenham Museum, Colonial Receipts

Take the whites of 24 eggs and a pound of double refined sugar beat and sifted fine; mix both together in a deep earthen pan, and with a whisk, whisk it well for two or three hours, till it looks white and thick, then with a thin broad board, or bunch of feathers, spread it all over the top and sides of the cake; set it at a proper distance before a clear fire to harden.

Frosting

Mrs. Dalrymple's Receipts, 1795

Whites of 8 eggs, 1/2 lb. sugar, beat 8 hours

NOTE: *By hand*

Clearing Sugar

E. Smith, 1729, The Compleat Housewife

Take two or three whites of Eggs and put them, in a Bason of Water, and with a very clean hand ladle that as you do Soup. Take nothing but the Froth, and when your Syrup boils, with a Ladle cover it with it; do this till your Syrup is clear, making still more Froth, and covering the syrup with it: it will make the worst Sugar as clear as any, and fit to preserve any Fruit.

Candying Angelica

E. Smith, 1729, The Compleat Housewife

Take Angelica that is young, and cut it in fit Lengths and boil it till it is pretty tender, keeping it close covered, then take it up and peel of all the strings; then put it in again, and let it simmer and scald till tis very green; then take it up and dry it in a Cloth and weigh it, and to every pound of Angelica take a pound of double-refined Sugar beated and sifted; put your Angelica in an earthen pot and strew the Sugar over it and let it stand two days: then boil it till it looks very clear, put it in a Colandar to drain the Syrups from it and take a little double refined Sugar and boil it to Sugar again; the throw in your Angelica and take it out in a little time, and put it on glass plates.

🐦🐦🐦

In winter, always set the handle of your pump as high as possible before you go to bed. Except in very rigid weather, this keeps the handle from freezing.

Mrs. Child, The American Frugal Housewife

Candying Flowers

Thomas Jenner, 1653, A Book of Fruits and Flowers

Gather your Flowers when dry; cut off the Leaves as far as the colour is good, according to your quantity, take of double-refined Sugar, and wet it with fair Water, and boil it to a candy height, then put in your Flowers, of what sort you please as Primroses, Violets, Cowslips, or Borage, with a Spoon; take them out as quick as you can, with as little of the Syrup, and may be and lay them in a dish over a gentle fire, and with a knife over a gentle fire spread them, that the Syrup may run from them; then change them upon another warm dish and when they are dry from the Syrup; have ready some double-refined Sugar, beated and sifted, and strew some on your Flowers; then take the Flowers in our Hands, and rub them gently in the hollow of your Hand and that will open the Leaves: a Stander-by strewing more sugar in your hand as you see convenient; so do until they are thoroughly open'd and dry; then put your Flowers in a dry Sieve and sift all the Sugar clean from them. They must be kept in a dry place. Rosemary Flower must be put whole into your Syrup. Young Mint Leaves you must open with your Fingers, but all Blossoms rub with your Hand as directed.

Brews

Hop Beer

Lucy Emerson, 1808, The New England Cookery

To make a barrel of beer, take five ounces of good hops, add two or three pails of water, simmer six hours strain this into your barrel when hot. Add  one gallon of molasses, stir this well together and then fill your barrel with water, stir the whole together. It will be fit for use in about forty -eight hours.

Ginger Beer

Amelia Simmons, 1796, American Cookery

Put into an earthen vessel 1 1/2 oz ginger 1 oz cream of tartar and 1 lb white sugar. Pour upon them 1 gal boiling water; when cold add 1 tablespoon yeast, let it stand till next morn. Bottle and keep in a cool place 3 days before you drink it. Be sure to use round corks and secure with twine or wire.

Mead

Amelia Simmons, 1796, American Cookery

Take 30 lb honey, 20 gallons of water hang it over the fire let it scald and the scum rise 2 hours boil it and skim 1 1/4 hour, let it stand in the same kettle till next day — ladle it off and take 1/2 oz cinnamon, a doz cloves, just break it and hang it in the bung let stand 10-12 day bottle for use.

Strawberry Wine

Sir Kenelme Digby, 1669, The Closet Open'd

Bruise the strawberries and put them into a Linnen-bag which hath been little used that so the Liquor may run through more easily. You hang in the bag at the bung into the vessel before you put in you Strawberries. The quantity of the fruit is left to your discretion for you will judge there to be enough of them when the color of the wine is high enough. During the working, you leave the bung open. The working being over, you stop your vessel. Cherry wine is made after the same fashion. But it is a little more trouble-some to break the Cherrystones.

Blackberry Cordial

Mrs. Dalrymple's Handwritten Receipts, 1795

To 1 lb juice, add 1 lb of loaf sugar and 1 qt brandy, boil until through skimmed, then bottle and rise. Raspberry is made the same.

Of *Rasbery Wine*

Elizabeth Wainwright, 1711, The Receipt Book of a Lady of the Reign of Queen Ann

Take ye frute full ripe, brus and strain ym, and to every gallan of juce put 2 pound of sugar. Put it in a barrill or pot and boung it close up. Let it stand a month or 5 weeks yn bottel it. Put in every bottel a lump of sugar. You may make chirey wine ye same way.

Clean a brass kettle before using it for cooking with salt and vinegar.

Mrs. Child, 1838, The American Frugal Housewife, dedicated to those who are not ashamed of economy

Coffee

Wenham Museum, Colonial Receipts

Allow two tablespoonsful for each person, grind it just before making, put it in a basin and break into it an egg yolk, white, shell, and all. Mix it up with the spoon to the consistency of mortar, put it in warm not boiling water in the coffee pot, let it boil up and break three times; then stand a few minutes and it will be as clear as amber and the egg will give it a rich taste.

Substitutes for Tea and Coffee

Several Ladies, 1805, The Pocumtuc Housewife

The leaves of currant bushes picked very small and dried on tin can hardly be distinguished from green tea. Peas roasted and ground are an excellent substitute for coffee and you would hardly know which was best.

Save all your fish skin, wash and dry it and keep to settle coffee.

Several Ladies, 1805, The Pocumtuc Housewife

Dr. Harvey's Pleasant Water-cider whereof he used to Drink Much

Sir Kenelme Digby, 1669, The Closet Open'd

Take one bushel of pippins cut them into slices with the Peelings and Cores: boil them in twelve gallons of water till the goodness of them be in the water, and that consumed about three gallons. Then strain it through a bag made of cotton: and when it is clear run out and almost cold, sweeten it with five pounds of Brown Sugar. Put a pint of Ale-yeast to it, and set it working two night and days. Then skim off the yeast clean, and put it into bottles, and let it stand two or three days till the yeast fall dead at the top.

Take this off clean with a knife and fill it up a little within the neck (so that a finger's breadth be empty below the stopple) and then stop the bottles and tie them, or else it will drive out the corks. Within a fortnight you may drink it: and it will keep five or six weeks.

To make *Tea with Eggs*

Sir Kenelme Digby, 1669, The Closet Open'd

To near a pint of the infusion of Tea, take two yolks of new-laid eggs, and beat them very well with a quantity of fine Sugar. When they are well incorporated pour your Tea on the Eggs and Sugar, stir them will together, and so drink it hot. This is when you come home from attending business abroad, are very hungry and yet have not convenience to eat presently a competent meal; it flyeth suddenly through the whole body and into the veins, and strentheneth exceedingly.

To make *a Fine Syllabub from the Cow*

Several Ladies, 1805, The Pocumtuc Housewife

Sweeten a quart of cider with double refined sugar. Grate nutmeg into it. Then milk your cow into your liquor. When you have thus added what quantity of milk you think proper, pour half a pint or more of the sweetest cream you get all over it.

❦❦❦

For anyone suspected of going into decline – Half a pint of milk, warm from the cow, made lusciously sweet with old conserve of roses and two tablespoons of the very best rum.
Take first thing in the morning.

Wenham Museum, Colonial Receipts

For *Entertaining the Minister* for an *Afternoon*

Wenham's Choice from Grandmother's Cookbook

Take a measure of each of sherry, port, and 1/2 measure of brandy. Put them in your best punch bowl with milk and sugar to taste. Stir well, and when it comes time to serve, add some well whipped cream, dust with nutmeg. Serve in your best glasses with small pieces of fruit cake.

Grandmother adds: "In olden time, instead of the whipped cream, the bowl was taken out to the cow and she was milked into the bowl until it was full of froth."

P.S. from Robert Edwards

"This is not as strange as it may seem. It was the daily custom to have syllabub at a home which I visited often just outside Media, Pennsylvania near Rose Tree Hunt Club. At late afternoon milking time there was a ceremony when the guests in the house collected in a group and partially filled tall glasses with the very finest Madeira and went in a procession to the cow barn (glasses in hand) where the milker would fill them with warm milk directly from the cow."

Preserves

Several Ladies, 1805, The Pocumtuc Housewife

Economical people will seldom use preserves except for sickness. They are unhealthy, expensive, and useless to those who are well. A pound of sugar to a pound of fruit is the rule for all preserves. The sugar should be melted over a moderate fire, skimmed clear and the fruit dropped in to simmer until it is soft. Put them in jars, lay a white paper thoroughly wet with brandy flat on the surface of the preserves. Cover tight from the air.

Cranberry Jelly

Mrs. Dalrymple's Handwritten Receipts, from 1795

2 qt cranberries, 1 of sugar, 1 of water, boil untill you think it will jelly. Try in a cup.

To make a conserve of *Barberies*

Thomas Dawson, 1597, The Second Part of the Good Hus-wives Jewell

Take your Barberies and picke them cleene, and set them over a soft fire, and put to them Rosewater as much as you think good, then when you thinke it be sodde enough, straine that, then seeth it againe, and to every pound of Barberies, one pound of suger, and meat you conserve.

Preserved Cranberries

Amelia Simmons, 1796, American Cookery

Wash and drain them and to each pound add 1 lb. loaf sugar. Dissolve the sugar in very little water, about 1/2 pint water to 1 lb. sugar and set it on the fire in a preserving kettle. Boil 10 minutes then put in your cranberries and boil slowly till quite soft and of a fine color.

Jely of Rasberys

Elizabeth Wainwright, 1711, The Receipt Book of a Lady of the Reign of Queen Ann

Brus & streane yr frut, boyl ye jues prety well, take to a pint of juce 2 qurters of a pound of sugar, boile ye sirop to a candy height yn put it into yr juge & boyl it to a jeley. Strean it into glasses.

To boile Sugar to a Candy Heght – To every pound of Sugar take half a pint of water, boile it together till it drows like a thred betwixt your finger and thumb.

To conserve *Cherries, Damesins or what Plummes all the Yeere in the Sirrop*

Thomas Dawson, 1597, The Second Part of the Good Hus-wives Jewell

First take faire water, so much as you shall think meete and one pound of sugar, and put them both into a faire bason and set the same over a soft fire till the sugar be melted, then pout thereto one pound and an halfe of chirries, or Damsons, and let them boile till they breake, then cover them in your galley pottes, and so keep them: this wise keeping propirtion in weight of Sugar and fruit, you may conserve as much as you list putting therto Sinamon and cloves, as aforesaid.

To pickle *Cucumbers in Slices*

E. Smith, 1729, The Complete Housewife or Accomplish'd Gentlewoman's Companion

Slice your Cucumber pretty thick and to a dozen of Cucumber slice in two or three good Onions and strew on them a large handful of Salt, and let them lie in their Liquor twenty-four hours; then strain them and put them between two coarse Cloths; then boil the best White-wine Vinegar, with some Cloves, Mace, and Jamaica Pepper in it, and pour it scalding hot over them, as much as will cover them all over; when they are cold, cover them up with Leather & and keep them for use.

To pickle *Dill and Collyflowers*

John Evelyn, Esq., 1699, A Herbal, A Discourse of Sallets

Boil the Collyflowers till they fall in pieces; then with some of the stalk and worst of the flower boil it in a part of the liquor till pretty strong. Then being taken off strain it; and when settled clean it from the bottom. Then with Dill, gross pepper, a pretty quantity of salt, when cold add as much vinegar as will make it sharp and pour upon the Collyflower.

❦❦❦

If females and children must wear cotton and linen dresses and aprons in winter, use the precaution to dip the dresses in strong alum water, after washing. This will prevent blazing if they catch fire.

To pickle *Mackrel*

E. Smith, 1729, The Compleat Housewife

Slit your Mackrel in halves, take out the Roes, gut and clean them, and strew Salt over them and lay one on another the Back of one to the Inside of the other, so let them lie two or three Hours then wipe every piece clean from the Salt and strew them over with Pepper beaten and grated Nutmeg, so let them be two or three Hours longer: then fry them well take them out of the Pan & lay them on coarse Cloths to drain; when cold put them in a Pan & cover them over with a Pickle of Vinegar boiled with Spice, when 'tis cold.

To make a conserve of *Roses,* and of any other Flowers

Thomas Dawson, 1597, The Second Part of the Good Hus-wives Jewell

Take your Roses before they be fullye sprung out, and chop off the white of them, and let the Roses be dried one day or two before they be stamped, and to one unce of these flowers take one unce and a halfe of fine beaten Sugar, and let your roses be beaten as you can, and after beat your roses and Sugar together againe, the put the Conserve into a faire glases: And likewise make all Conserve of Flowers.

To pickle *Nasturtium Buds*

E. Smith, 1729, The Compleat Housewife or Accomplish'd Gentlewoman's Companion

Gather your little Knobs quickly after your Blossoms are off: put them in cold Water and Salt for three days, shifting them once a day; then make a Pickle (but do not boil it at all) of some White-wine, some White-wine Vinegar, Eschalot, Horse-radish, Pepper, Salt, Cloves, and Mace whole, and Nutmeg quartered; then put in your Seeds and stop them close; they are to be eaten as Capers.

Lamps will have a less disagreeable smell if you dip your wick yarn in strong hot vinegar, & dry it.

Mrs. Child, 1830, The Frugal Housewife

Glossary

Definitions from the Compact Edition of the *Oxford English Dictionary*.

Ambergrease – a wax-like substance of marbled ashy colour, found floating in tropical seas and as a morbid secretion in the intestines of the sperm-whale. It is odoriferous and used in perfumery, formerly in cookery.

Bason – basin, a circular vessel of greater width than depth with sloping or curving sides

Bilge – side

Brawn – muscle

Bung – a large cork stopper for the mouth of a cask

Caudle – a warm drink consisting of thin gruel mixed with wine or ale sweetened and spiced given chiefly to sick people, especially women in childbed; also to their visitors

Charvil – Chervil

Coffin – a mould of paste for a pie

Collyflower – cauliflower

Crums – Crumbs

Currans – currants also corants

Cullender – colander

Eschalot – shallot

Farce – to stuff, to fill full of something

French Manchet – the finest kind of wheaten bread

Froiz – a kind of pancake or omelette often containing bits of bacon

Gammon – the ham of a swine

Gill – 1/4 of a pint i.e. 1/2 cup

Hoop – deep round cake pan with a removeable bottom and a spring clip fastener

Lettice – lettuce

Limon – lemon

March-pane – marzipan

Pap – pulp of apple when roasted

Pipkin – small earthenware cooking pot

Pippin – apple

Pruans – prunes

Runnet – rennet, mass of curdled milk found in the stomach of an unweaned calf or other animal, used for curdling milk in making cheese – also a preparation of the inner membrane of the stomach used for this purpose

Sack – a general name for a class of white wine formerly imported from Spain and the Canaries

Saleratus – an impure bicarbonate of potash much used as an ingredient in baking powders

Sallet – salad, or vegetable, also sallad

Searce – to strain

Sinamon – cinnamon, also cinamon and cinamom

Sippet – a small piece of toasted or fired bread usually served in soup or broth or with meat or used for dipping in gravy; a small sop

Sodden – boiled or cooked by boiling

Soop – soup

Sop – piece of bread or the like dropped or steeped in water, wine, etc, before being eaten or cooked

Spareges, sperage, sparragrass – asparagus

Spinage spinnage, spinnach – spinach

Spitchcocked – an eel cut into pieces dressed with breadcrumbs and chopped herbs, broiled or fired

Sweetmeates – sweet foods such as sugared cakes or pastry confectionery

Umblers – digestible insides

Vergious, verjuice, verdjice – the acid juice of green or unripe grapes, crab apples or other sour fruit pressed and formed into a liquor, much used in cooking as a condiment

Walm – boiling

Yn – then

"Temper lies in the stomach."

Mrs Horace Mann, Christianity in the Kitchen